SHORT • SCENIC • WALKS

WHARFE

GW00375252

PAUL HANNON

HILLSIDE PUBLICATIONS
2 New School Lane, Cullingworth, Bradford BD13 5DA

First Published 2020   © Paul Hannon 2020

ISBN 978 1 907626 24 1

Sketch maps based on OS 1947 1-inch maps

Cover illustrations: Linton; Burnsall
Back cover: Cow & Calf Rocks; Page 1: Littondale near Litton
(Paul Hannon/Yorkshire Photo Library)

Printed in China on behalf of Latitude Press

HILLSIDE GUIDES... cover much of Northern England

• 50 Yorkshire Walks For All   • Journey of the Wharfe (photobook)

Short Scenic Walks • Wharfedale & Ilkley • Harrogate & Nidderdale
• North York Moors • Ambleside & South Lakeland • Teesdale & Weardale
• Bowland & Ribble Valley • Aire Valley • Haworth • Hebden Bridge
• Upper Wensleydale • Lower Wensleydale • Swaledale • Malhamdale
• Sedbergh & Dentdale • Ingleton & Western Dales • Around Pendle

Walking in Yorkshire   • Wharfedale & Malham
• North York Moors South & West   • North York Moors North & East
• Nidderdale & Ripon   • Three Peaks & Howgill Fells
• Harrogate & Ilkley   • Wensleydale & Swaledale
• Aire Valley & Bronte Country   • Howardian Hills & Vale of York
• Yorkshire Wolds   • Calderdale & South Pennines
• South Yorkshire   • West Yorkshire Countryside

Lancashire/North Pennines
• Bowland • Pendle & the Ribble • Eden Valley • Alston & Allendale

Visit us at www.hillsidepublications.co.uk

CONTENTS

Hebden Gill
Starbotton

INTRODUCTION

Wharfedale is one of the major valleys of the Yorkshire Dales, and these 30 walks explore it from the gateway town of Ilkley to the heart of the national park beyond Buckden. This beautiful valley is probably the most popular in the Dales, being very accessible from the cities of Leeds and Bradford and their surrounding towns. The lovely Wharfe is formed by the confluence of Oughtershaw Beck and Greenfield Beck, and its delectable opening miles are known as Langstrothdale. Its major tributary is the Skirfare, which flows through Littondale to lose its identity near Kilnsey.

The Wharfe flows by a string of delightful villages including Kettlewell, Burnsall and Appletreewick. Fascinating limestone landmarks include Trollers Gill, Conistone Dib and Kilnsey Crag, while notable historical features include Bolton Priory, Barden Tower, Parcevall Hall and Yockenthwaite stone circle. The gritstone heights of Barden Moor and Barden Fell face each other across the Wharfe, overlooking mercurial riverside paths between Bolton Abbey and Grassington. Much evidence of 19th century lead mining survives in spoil heaps, smelt mills and kilns, shafts and levels. Ilkley is best known for the celebrated Ilkley Moor, whose gritstone crags are best seen at the iconic Cow & Calf Rocks. The moor is also dotted with early man's stone circles, burial cairns and the cup & ring markings that decorate many a dark boulder. In reality, Ilkley Moor is but one part of the great sweep of Rombalds Moor.

The majority of walks are on rights of way or established access areas and paths: a handful which cross Open Access land are noted as such. Most days of the year you can freely walk here, but dogs are banned from grouse moors other than on rights of way. These areas can occasionally be closed, most likely from the grouse-shooting season's August start, though weekends should largely be unaffected: details from Natural England and information centres. Whilst the route description should be sufficient to guide you around, a map is recommended for greater information and interest: Ordnance Survey Explorer maps OL2, OL30 and 297 cover the walks.

●Yorkshire Dales National Park
Yoredale, Bainbridge, Leyburn DL8 3EL (0300-456 0030)
●Grassington National Park Centre (01756-751690)
●Information Centre, Station Road, Ilkley (01943-436232)
●Tourist Information, Coach Street, Skipton (01756-792809)

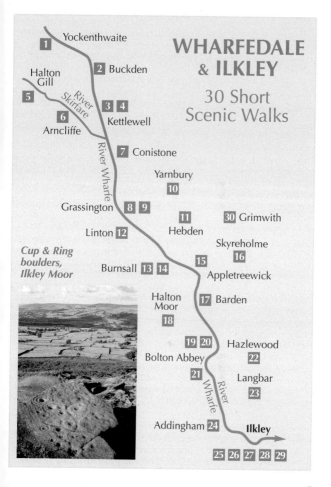

1 Yockenthwaite

WHARFEDALE & ILKLEY

30 Short Scenic Walks

2 Buckden

Halton Gill

River Skirfare

5

6

Arncliffe

3 **4**

Kettlewell

7 Conistone

River Wharfe

Yarnbury

10

Grassington **8** **9**

11 **30** Grimwith

Linton **12**

Hebden

Skyreholme

16

Cup & Ring boulders, Ilkley Moor

Burnsall **13** **14**

15

Appletreewick

Halton Moor

17 Barden

18

19 **20**

Hazlewood

22

Bolton Abbey

21

River Wharfe

Langbar

23

Addingham **24**

Ilkley

25 **26** **27** **28** **29**

3¹₂ miles from Yockenthwaite

A classic section of riverbank is equalled by a gentle higher level return with great views

Start Yockenthwaite Bridge (SD 904790; BD23 5JH), roadside parking upstream
Map OS Explorer 30, Yorkshire Dales North/Central

This uppermost section of the Wharfe above Hubberholme is known as Langstrothdale, its regularly spaced settlements being backdrop to mile upon mile of unsurpassed river scenery. Much of the upper dale came into the care of the National Trust in the 1990s. Leave the road by crossing slender Yockenthwaite Bridge into the farming hamlet in a magnificent setting. 'Eogan's clearing' was named by the Norsemen who settled here: much later, all this area was part of the hunting forest of Langstrothdale Chase.

Cross the bridge and up the track into the hamlet, but without rising to the main buildings, turn right at the first fork on a track above the lowest buildings. Pass through a gate and a couple more into the field behind, then down to a stile just below. From here a path slants down to join the riverbank. Note the lively appearance of a spring, swelling into the river from directly under the bank. The path now shadows the Wharfe downstream in idyllic surroundings, never more than a few steps from its bank. Passing through several fields, a tighter enclosed spell opens out into fields again to see the skyline of Buckden Pike filling the frame ahead.

Just beyond a barn the path rises a few strides to negotiate Strans Gill by way of a footbridge. An initially firmer path resumes, and at the end the path slants a little left to a wall-stile just above. A lovely final open stretch culminates in a rebuilt path across a steep, scrubby bank, emerging from undergrowth to reveal Hubberholme church tower in front. The path runs on to meet your return track just behind the church. Turn right through the gate between church and farm to have a look at this tiny settlement with church and pub separated by the bridge. For a note on Hubberholme see page 9.

From the church return through the gate, and this time follow the broad access road rising up the extensive pasture to ultimately climb more steeply to its terminus at isolated Scar House, scene of early Quaker gatherings. Rising between the buildings you emerge onto the base of the open fell. Here turn left to a stile by a gate, from where a sketchy path sets an obvious level course through the minor outcrops of a limestone shelf. Throughout this section you enjoy largely level walking with some outstanding views over the youthful Wharfe in Langstrothdale to the Birks Fell ridge opposite.

Entering a small wood, the path soon leaves by re-crossing Strans Gill, a normally dry limestone ravine beneath which lurks a complex cave system. The path then drops half-left to a stile before commencing a level course through numerous walls in various condition. Further, beyond a bridle-gate, Yockenthwaite appears ahead, and a very short way further a guidepost indicates a gap in the abandoned wall on your left: here the path makes a sustained slant to a wall at the bottom. It then runs on beneath trees to emerge via a bridle-gate onto a track above Yockenthwaite. This takes you back down to the hamlet to finish.

The Wharfe below Yockenthwaite

5 miles from Buckden

Easy walking through memorable upper dale scenery linking three settlements

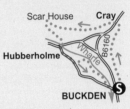

Start Village centre (SD 942772; BD23 5JA), National Park car park
Map OS Explorer 30, Yorkshire Dales North/Central

Buckden is the first sizeable settlement encountered by the Wharfe, and was the centre of a medieval hunting forest - the Buck Inn recalls this importance. There are also tearooms, shop and WC. Leave the car park by a gate at its northern end, from where a stony track gently rises up Buckden Rake. This section of Roman road remains to this day an excellent route, providing a perfect picture of the dalehead, looking past Hubberholme into Langstrothdale.

At the end of the surround of trees it turns right through a gate to commence a pleasant level section. Ignore an early track curving up right, and further on ignore a path bound for Buckden Pike which also strikes off right. A splendid green stroll ensues, and just after the adjacent wall returns after an absence, take an easily missed bridle-gate in it to drop down a steep field alongside a wall. At the bottom a gate leads to the sidestream of Cray Gill, which is crossed by stepping-stones to join the road alongside the White Lion pub in the farming hamlet of Cray.

Depart by a farm track immediately behind the pub, and follow it up to the left: keep right at a very early fork to pass through a natural limestone floored farmyard above various farm buildings. A little waterfall tumbles to your right as you cross its stream near the end of the yard. Ignoring a path signed down to the left, pass through a gate above the last buildings. A sketchy way remains level through two fields before swinging right towards a barn ahead. Through a gate to its left, swing further right to a tiny footbridge over the ravine of Crook Gill.

From the footbridge swing left to commence a dead-flat, easy mile on short-cropped turf above a well-defined escarpment cloaked in trees on the left. The slopes above rise to 2109ft/643m on unfrequented Yockenthwaite Moor. With just one intervening stile, all too soon the path arrives above isolated Scar House, scene of early Quaker gatherings. Turn down between the buildings onto the stony access road down the hillside into Hubberholme.

This humble hamlet boasts two famous buildings and a shapely bridge connecting them. St Michael's is a gem, its tower showing Norman traces. Best feature is a 500-year old oak rood loft, one of only two remaining in Yorkshire, while some pews bear the trademark of the Kilburn workshops of 'Mousy' Thompson. Directly over the river is the homely George Inn in an idyllic setting. This was Bradford writer J B Priestley's favourite corner, small wonder that he chose to have his ashes scattered here. Cross the bridge over the Wharfe to the pub, and turn left along the road, passing Kirkgill Manor. After about half a mile a gate on the left sends a short track to the riverbank, where a firm path runs a lovely course on an embankment downstream to Buckden Bridge. Join the road to re-cross the Wharfe back into the village.

Hubberholme church

4½ miles from Kettlewell

Easy riverbank walking to a lovely village, with a delightful, slightly elevated return

Start *Village centre (SD 968722; BD23 5QX), National Park car park*
Map *OS Explorer 30, Yorkshire Dales North/Central*

Kettlewell is the principal village of the upper dale, with the Blue Bell, Racehorses and Kings Head supported by tearooms and shop. Kettlewell found 21st century fame as principal location for the movie 'Calendar Girls'. St Mary's church takes a back seat, with stocks and maypole nearby. Leave by crossing the bridge on the Wharfe at the village entrance. From a gate on the right a track heads away, but before it enters a field, turn down a path to the riverbank. Soon deflected away along a fieldside by bridle-gates in a wall, the river is quickly rejoined on an initially firm path. A brief walled section joins a broader cart track past a barn, quickly emerging into open fields amid archetypal Dales scenery.

Rapidly becoming enclosed by walls, this runs for some time before ending in a field. A grassy continuation runs through several fields, then later ignore the wallside way ahead towards a barn, and take a broad path bearing right to rejoin the wall to lead to the river. A briefly enclosed section avoids an eroded riverbank, past which a bridle-gate sees the river turn away. Continue ahead to a wall-stile, and a clear path runs on as the river immediately returns at a plank on a streamlet. The Wharfe again plays cat-and-mouse, bending sharply away: with a crumbling wall on your left, cross a pasture to find the river again. At a slight rise to a pair of gates, the right one sends a path briefly on a little bank above the river. Dropping to a streamlet bridge and on to a gate/stile, the grassy path finds the river again, this time tracing it upstream through several small pastures to a sturdy footbridge across it.

Cross the bridge and follow the walled track away to a gate onto the road at the entrance to Starbotton. Go briefly left to the Fox & Hounds, focal point of this unassuming village. Starbotton stands on its own swift-flowing beck, which in 1686 was swollen by a deluge causing disastrous floods. After the pub turn right to a junction by a bridge on the beck, then turn right to pass some lovely corners hiding 17th century cottages. Passing the old school house you quickly return to the village edge. Your departure is through a gate on the left just before rejoining the valley road.

A grassy path heads away through a gateway to a gate just beyond. Through it, ascend the field to a stile in the top wall. Turn right on a grassy path above it, this same path leading unfailingly all the way back. This superb, near-level ramble enjoys glorious views over the valley to Old Cote Moor. The path crosses several pastures beneath woodland with springtime bluebells. Beyond the wood, Kettlewell appears not too far ahead. The path drops a little to run closer to the wall below. Beneath a small wood above the village school, further pastures are crossed before dropping down a tapering corner on the village edge. Through a gap-stile at the bottom, a short enclosed way drops down to a back road in the village. Go left to a crossroads by the shop, then over the bridge in front. Turn right between the church and the Kings Head, keeping right at the maypole junction to return to the start.

Wharfedale between Kettlewell and Starbotton

DOWBER GILL

3³4 miles from Kettlewell

**An intimate beckside ramble
with a contrastingly open return**

Hag Dyke

B6160 Wharfe

Dowber Gill

X Providence Pot

S

KETTLEWELL

***Start** Village centre (SD 968722;
BD23 5QX), National Park car park*
***Map** OS Explorer 30, Yorkshire Dales North/Central*

From the car park head into the village, and leave the main road for one to the right before the bridge by the Racehorses and Blue Bell hotels. Fork left at the maypole to pass the church, and at the Kings Head turn right on a lane alongside Cam Gill Beck. At a bridge and former chapel the lane becomes a track, and a little further it crosses inflowing Dowber Gill Beck. Here turn up a little beckside path to a stile in the wall. Now turn right to begin a long mile and a quarter in close company with the beck.

After an early ladder-stile a grand path runs on into the side valley's tight confines. It's just you and the stream, enjoying little waterslides over rocky shelves: though the path is occasionally faint, it's impossible to go astray. Great Whernside's upper slopes appear on the skyline ahead. Further, a low cliff directly above the path unleashes a sizeable spring, gushing out to supply the greater part of the beck: above here its course can be bone-dry. Virtually no height is gained until the unmistakable site of Providence Pot is reached, either by crossing the beck just before it, or remaining more enterprisingly on the left bank. Sited in the stream, it is key to a famous underground system where Dowbergill Passage links with Dow Cave to the north: a manhole cover guards the vertical shaft. The slopes above are scarred with old lead workings.

Just behind is the meeting of twin becks beneath rougher slopes, but your path is a clear one rising left through bracken alongside the pothole. Higher up, the path takes advantage of a distinctive dry ditch to ascend by. This soon levels out to reveal bouldery Hag Dyke Edge up ahead, with Great Whernside's high summit ridge back to the right; then just ahead, Hag Dyke itself. Advance on a thin path to the building. From a gate by sheep pens a small gate at the far side of the building sees you emerge at the front. At 1510ft/460m this is one of the country's highest buildings, and since 1947 has been put to use as a scouts' outdoor centre.

Follow the access track out to a gate, then leave it for an inviting broad, grassy path dropping half-left. At once its course down splendid rough-grass pastures can be discerned almost all the way, keeping for the most part just above the well-defined drop to your outward route. The path drops through a collapsed wall and down to a small gate, along a wallside to a stile and on to another small gate. As the wall climbs away and open slopes take over, the path is now firmly atop the steep drop to Dowber Gill.

A marker post on the end reveals more of the village, and just beneath it take the main, right fork to slant away from the gill. Dropping to a gate/stile, it winds down more steeply to a gate in a wall below. Continue down and across to a wall-stile, through which a super green way curves down a final pasture to meet the outward route at Dowber Gill Beck. The finish can be varied by crossing the bridge and taking an enclosed path right of the old chapel. This runs between gardens and houses to join a short access track, emerging onto the parallel back road to go left into the centre.

Dowber Gill

4½ miles from Halton Gill

Easy walking by riverbank and limestone flanks in a remote corner of the Dales

Start Village centre (SD 880764;
BD23 5QN), parking area by green
Map OS Explorer 30, Yorkshire Dales North/Central

Halton Gill is the first settlement in Littondale, its cluster of buildings including an old chapel and grammar school. From the junction by the green turn down the Stainforth road over Halton Gill Bridge, and a stile on the right sends steps down to the river. Follow the Skirfare upstream through gates and stiles. After a pair of plank bridges over springs, take a bridle-gate in the adjacent fence to resume upstream through another. The bank opens out to give super rambling, with a fine moment where the river tumbles over limestone ledges. A little further, the path squeezes past sheep pens to emerge onto a road at Foxup Bridge, where the streams of Foxup Beck and Cosh Beck combine to create the Skirfare.

Go briefly left and take a gate set back opposite Foxup Bridge Farm. A grassy track winds up the field to the right-hand of two gates, with big views back over the farm's remote setting. The way ascends a large, steep pasture: ignoring a less obvious right branch towards a gate in the right-hand wall, continue up the grassy track. It levels out to contour left to a corner gate, through which head away above the left-hand wall. This drops away but leaves a broad, grassy path marching on. Grand views look down the dale and across to Halton Gill beneath Horse Head Moor. Remaining level, a large pasture is crossed to another gate, continuing above the minor outcrops of Hesleden Bergh to meet the Stainforth road.

Turn right along the open road, with the side valley of Penyghent Gill ahead beneath Fountains Fell. Beyond a cattle-grid Penyghent majestically appears ahead. Approaching a fence coming up from the left, a guidepost sends a thin trod doubling back left.

This quickly drops onto a broad green way, but as you set off left along it, shortly drop briefly right onto a parallel green way with the fence just a short way below. Resume left on this lower way, with a modest scar below you. Soon reaching the beginnings of a substantial limestone scar, the way swings left: instead drop right the very short way to the fence, where a good path has now formed. Resume left on this above fine gill scenery deep below. Your gently declining path merges into a cart track dropping from the left, and together you drop the short way further to a corner gate. A green track slants down towards the farm at Nether Hesleden, passing through a gate between houses.

Go left along the front of one bearing a 1748 datestone, and follow the drive out the few steps to a gate. Just past it take a stile on the left, and continue briefly parallel with the drive before slanting left up to bridle-gates on an access track. Just beyond is a wall-stile, from where head away with a fence. Continue across the field centre to a gate, and on in the same fashion to another in front of a tumbledown barn: Halton Gill is revealed ahead. Passing to its right, the largely faint path commences a course through a number of stile/gate combinations, regularly shadowed by the chain of Heber Side Barns to your left. Ultimately passing through a gate, a wall on your left ushers the way gently right, down to the riverbank. This ensures a fine finish for the few minutes upstream back to Halton Gill Bridge.

Halton Gill

4¾ miles from Arncliffe

Delectable rambling on valley paths throughout this flattest of walks

Start Village centre (SD 931718; BD23 5QE), roadside parking
Map OS Explorer 30, Yorkshire Dales North/Central

Arncliffe is one of Yorkshire's most attractive villages, its Falcon Inn and characterful houses stood back from a spacious green. St Oswald's church with its 500-year old tower occupies a beautiful riverside setting. From the green head west on the Malham road, and after the bridge on Cowside Beck take a walled track in front. This ends at a stile by the right-hand of two gates into a field where stone flags negotiate a moist corner. Cross to a stile near the left corner, then cross a vast field where a wooden slab bridges a streamlet from one of several springs over to the left.

Through a gate behind, the path bears gently right to approach the Skirfare, its bed normally dry due to the river taking a subterranean course further upstream. Advancing on, the river briefly wanders off. Continue through a gateway in an old wall, on through a gap-stile in a corner and on to a gate/stile into Scoska Wood. The steep wooded slopes of this nature reserve support the largest surviving natural ash and rowan wood in the Dales. The riverbed curves back in to join the grassy path, which leaves the reserve through a stile to which you will return. For now, cross the riverbed at some massive stone blocks, only impassable in spate.

Across, resume upstream on a good path on the wooded bank to quickly reach an impasse. A bridle-gate takes you away from the river on an inviting walled path. This swings left, and before long leave by a stile on the right to follow a right-hand wall to a stile in it. Continue on the other side to a stile back onto the enclosed footway. Go straight on it to quickly abandon it again, at a bridle-gate and kissing-gate into a field on the left. A gate at the far end accesses another walled way, little more than footpath width. Further, cross a track passing between fields, and just ahead, again continue along a narrow walled way. When it swings sharp right to become overgrown, a stile escapes into a field on the left. Cross to a wall-stile just ahead, then bear right across a larger field to a small gate onto the road entering Litton.

Passing the Queens Arms, go left through the small village, and leave the road down a drive to the left opposite a small green after the phonebox. Bear left of a wall at lovely Elbeck House to a footbridge on the normally still dry river. Turn left to a stile and across to a small gate at the end. Turn right with a streamlet, crossing a wooden bridge onto a track. Just a few steps left, take a gate on the right. Cross the field to a gateway then go left with the wall, continuing to a corner bridle-gate to rejoin the tree-lined riverbed. A path squeezes downstream with a lichen-covered wall, emerging at a gate to resume through fields. Through an old wall the river bends away a little: cross a streamlet at a stone slab and through a long field centre to a bend of the river. The outward route is rejoined by passing through a small gate in the fence alongside the stepping-stones. Return to Arncliffe the way you came.

Arncliffe

3 miles from Conistone

A superb limestone ravine leads to a classic Upper Wharfedale viewpoint

Start Village centre (SD 980674; BD23 5HS), limited parking, further room on wide section of road towards bridge
Map OS Explorer 2, Yorkshire Dales South/West

Conistone is an attractive little village avoided by the main road which heads up-dale across the river at Kilnsey, famed for the stupendous Kilnsey Crag. Conistone's central junction features a small refuge in which to relax beneath a tall maypole: close by is a pony trekking centre. Every block of stone in Conistone's many old cottages neatly matches the natural landscape of the village's hinterland. The hidden church of St Mary retains some Norman features, though most poignant is a churchyard memorial to the six victims of the Mossdale Cavern potholing disaster of 1967.

From the main junction set off along the Kettlewell road, then immediately turn right on a track across a wide green. From a gate at the far end a path becomes stony underfoot as it enters Conistone Dib, a classic example of a dry limestone valley. After being tightly confined by the imposing buttresses of Gurling Trough the path emerges into the open, and on through a bridle-gate to pass through a long, green pasture. From a bridle-gate near the end the slopes close in again for a short, stony climb to the valley head. At the very top the wall is crossed by a tiny gate as it abuts onto a cliff, and you must undertake a minor scramble. From a kissing-gate on the right just above, join a path that immediately passes left through a bridle-gate and very briefly on between walls to a gate accessing the firm track of Bycliffe Road.

Turn right for a couple of minutes to an outer wall corner on the left, then go left with the wall the few strides to see a circular dewpond. This is one of many in these parts created to slake the thirsts of cattle on these dry limestone uplands. Now retrace steps briefly to a grassy way dropping right off Bycliffe Road, and heading directly away. Before long a thinner branch bears left to a well-preserved limekiln beneath a cairned knoll. Resume on your grassy way left of the kiln, swinging right between a limestone pavement on your left and the knoll on your right. As pavement and knoll fade, your way drops slightly and crosses a broader green way to reach a wall-stile in front of the rocky knoll of Conistone Pie.

Cross the stile to access the 'Pie', a conspicuous Wharfedale landmark. It commands a superb view of the fork of the arrow-like valleys of the Wharfe and the Skirfare, emerging from Littondale. Across the valley is Kilnsey Crag, while on the dale floor is Amerdale Dub, confluence of the Skirfare with the Wharfe. Re-cross the stile and follow the inviting grassy path ahead. Keep left at an early fork to run beneath a modest limestone scar, and quickly returning to Bycliffe Road above Conistone Dib. Turn sharp right on it - now as Scot Gate Lane - through a gate to descend Wassa Bank past a mast. This affords views into your opening mile in Conistone Dib, while the Kilnsey scene appears ahead. Becoming fully enclosed at a gate, the access road leads down to join the Kettlewell road. Turn left into the village, passing the church en route.

In Conistone Dib

4½ miles from Grassington

A splendid woodland nature reserve followed by a lovely riverbank stroll

Start *Village centre (SE 002639; BD23 5AD), National Park car park*
Map *OS Explorer 2, Yorkshire Dales South/West*

From the square head up the street past the Devonshire Arms to a crossroads by the Devonshire Institute. Here turn left on Chapel Street, and part way on turn right up Bank Lane, which quickly loses its surface and swings left as a walled track. At a path junction towards the end, turn left through a small gate, over a plank bridge and across the field to a stile. Now go left a short way down to another stile. While the Dales Way goes right on the track here, simply cross to a stile in the wall opposite. Bear right across a large, undulating field to a similar stile onto an enclosed track, Cove Lane. Ahead is a fine arrangement of field walls and barns in front of Grass Wood. Accompany the green lane to its demise, and from the right-hand gate, cross to the far end of the field and on to a wall-stile into Grass Wood. This largest surviving broadleaved woodland in the Dales hosts a bewildering variety of flowers.

A good path heads up through the trees, keeping right on a broader path at the first fork. The path rises steadily for some time to a brow near a wall corner. The now level, broad, firmer path runs through a clearing by a distinctive trough to a cross-paths. The thin path left offers a couple of minutes' diversion up a low limestone scar to Fort Gregory, an Iron Age hillfort from AD70. Back at the cross-paths resume on the main path, now broadening into a track. However, quickly approaching a broader clearing, leave the track for a less firm path branching right. It maintains a level course through trees with a moss-covered limestone pavement on the left, before descending towards the far end of the wood. After a sharp left turn the descent gathers pace, merging into the wide track from earlier. Continuing down with the boundary wall close to hand, the track deposits you onto Grass Wood Lane.

Turn left for a few minutes until a gate on the right into Lower Grass Wood. Of several paths heading away, take the main one bearing left along the wood edge: soon forking, the right branch takes you down to the bank of the Wharfe. Heading downstream a super path soon rises onto a higher bank to merge with another path. Further, at an angled cross-paths on a knoll, bear right on the main one back down to the river and on to reach a kissing-gate out of the wood. Some delightful riverbank walking on open pastures leads to a wooded knoll.

Here at Ghaistrill's Strid the river is channelled through a ravine: this takes all the water when the river is low, otherwise the Wharfe rushes through and over rocky shelves alongside. The path runs to a ladder-stile ahead, into a short enclosed spell above the lively river. A couple of stiles further the riverbank is regained. Through a couple of small gates resume along the riverbank, and on bridging a sidestream Grassington Bridge appears ahead. On approaching it the path bears left to rise to a gate onto the B6265. Turn up the roadside footway to finish.

Ghaistrill's Strid

4³4 miles from Grassington

Lush limestone pastures, extensive views and rich history above Grassington

Start Village centre (SE 002639; BD23 5AD), National Park car park
Map OS Explorer 2, Yorkshire Dales South/West

Grassington is a thriving community with pubs, cafes and shops. The cobbled square with its folk museum is focal point, but hidden away is enough interest for a day's leisurely exploration. From the square head up the street past the Devonshire Arms to a crossroads by the Devonshire Institute, and turn left on Chapel Street. Part way on turn right up Bank Lane, which quickly swings left as a walled track. Remain on this to its demise at a gate/stile, from where an inviting green way ascends the slender field. When it opens out at a wall corner, remain with the right-hand wall to slant to the far end. You are now on Kimpergill Hill, surrounded by barely discernible ancient settlements and field systems.

From the stile at the very end resume with the wall on your right, slanting across to a stile in the wall above. The good path maintains this slant through successive old walls, a stile just behind, and on further across a larger pasture. Half way on it slants to a stile in the wall above, following the left-hand option to rise diagonally again across another sizeable pasture. Here you pass a walled dewpond: once a water source for cattle, it is now dry. From a stile at the end the path soon reveals the isolated former farm and drovers' inn of Bare House just two minutes ahead.

From a gate to its left swing right outside the small enclosure behind, a grassy track curving around outside the wall to roofless High Barn. From a gate alongside, a track crosses the field to a gate onto Downs Pasture. Bear right on this now firm track rising to a gate ahead. This admits to a walled green lane, a splendid stride over the walk's high point. This leads all the way to Old Moor Lane on the edge of Yarnbury. En route, a smelt mill chimney stands tall on Grassington Moor, while at a sharp bend Yarnbury appears just ahead. Also, Mossy Moor Reservoir is seen beneath the gnarled crest of more distant Simon's Seat: beneath you are distinctive bell pits from lead mining days. Turn right onto Moor Lane at Yarnbury. Just before the surfaced lanehead, the way bridges a tunnel through which ore was hauled from a deep mine level. Yarnbury House was the 19th century mine agent's office.

From a stile on the left after the houses, a faint trod crosses to a stile in the opposite wall, left of a gate. Bear gently right up to a wall-stile to emerge by the distinctive banks of an ancient circular henge. Resume to the far corner, where a stile re-admits onto Moor Lane. Turn left, and just after Mire House on the left, take a stile on the right. A trod crosses to a gate/stile in the wall ahead, revealing a Grassington district panorama. A path descends the steeper slopes of Pasture Wood to a stile in the wall below. A grassy way continues down to a corner gate then resume on the wallside, over a stile and on past Intake Lathe to a gate. Grassy Intake Lane is joined, dropping to an access road at some houses. Either go left down it, or from a stile opposite descend a snicket onto the foot of Bank Lane. Retrace steps back into the centre.

Grassington

4¹⁄2 miles from Yarnbury

Grassington Moor

Absorbing lead mining remains in a bleak upland setting

Yarnbury

x chimney

Cupola Corner

Hebden Gill

Start Yarnbury House, 1¹⁄2 miles up Moor Lane out of Grassington (SE 015658; BD23 5EQ), parking at road end
Map OS Explorer 2, Yorkshire Dales South/West
• Open Access land, no dogs: see page 4

Grassington Moor was a major lead mining centre: the industry peaked in the early 19th century, and ended completely before that century did. At some 1150ft/350m up, Yarnbury's bleak setting would have been much busier when Yarnbury House was the mine agent's office. From the road end turn right over the cattle-grid and head away on the hard track of Duke's New Road into the mining site, with Low Grinding Mill on your left. Advance along the track for a few minutes to reach a horse whim on your right, where horses trod circles to lift ore and spoil up the shaft.

Here leave the track and drop past the pit to a wall junction. Through the old stile cross to a sandy area, and ignoring the wall-stile in front, go left the short way to an old stile at the corner. Leaving the site behind head away with a crumbling wall to a stile at the end, and a thin path crosses a rough pasture. A knoll on your left features a ruined hut enclosing a deep, covered shaft. Ignoring the path's swing left, cross to a wall-stile ahead, and cross a reedy pasture. Crossing a grassy track, advance to a stile ahead. Bear gently right, crossing an access road, with stakes guiding the thin trod to a stile in the far wall. Resume the direction, crossing to a gate in the wall ahead: in this pasture you encounter sections of old water leats. Through the gate turn left on a broad grassy way between walls. Emerging, continue down the wallside, looking across Hebden Gill to the deep cleft of Bolton Gill. The final stage is enclosed again as the track zigzags down onto the gill floor.

Through the gate turn left, immediately through another gate and along the firm track. This twice fords the tiny beck, pulls through mining debris, drops again, then ascends past a limekiln. Climbing out of the gill to a fork, go right through a gate, ascending gently to a gateway. Extensive spoil heaps to the left incorporate the Wheel House and the near-300ft deep Beever's Engine Shaft. Through the gateway the track rises to meet Duke's New Road. Turn right to a gate/stile onto Grassington Moor, and the track swings round over the embankment of an old dam at the upper reach of the gill. Approaching a gate/stile at Cupola Corner, instead take a grassy branch right to Cupola Smelt Mill, where a stile puts you into the old site. From here a mile-long system of flues took fumes to the lofty chimney that is your next objective. Go left a few strides to rejoin the hard track, but at the first bend leave by a grassier way bearing right. Quickly turn left to ascend alongside the flue to the preserved chimney at the top, a major landmark.

Resume on a path gently rising the short way to the nearest spoil heaps, revealing Coalgrovebeck Reservoir. Go left on the dam edge path and drop down a groove to High Winding House. On its other side briefly cross open ground to a hard track, and go a short way right to a crossroads of such tracks. Turn left, winding around through extensive spoil heaps to swing left and slowly drop down out of the workings. The Duke's Water Course is crossed to a gate where your track becomes enclosed as Old Moor Lane. Simply follow its wide walled course down to a dip before a steady rise over the brow to reveal Yarnbury. Just before the end you bridge a tunnel where ore was hauled from a mine level.

Smelt mill chimney,
Grassington Moor

3¹2 miles from Hebden

Good paths discover a fascinating lead mining past in a colourful side valley

Start Top end of village (SE 026631; BD23 5DE) where main street joins B6265, roadside parking

Map OS Explorer 2, Yorkshire Dales South/West

Hebden is a small village with the Clarendon pub, tearoom and St Peter's church. Like neighbouring Grassington it grew with the lead mining industry, with Hebden Gill rich in evidence. From Town Hill crossroads below the pub, take the unsigned road north above Hebden Beck. This remains surfaced to its demise at Hole Bottom. As it swings left go straight ahead through a gate alongside cottages, and a track runs out into the open surrounds of Hebden Gill. Quickly crossing a charming stone-arched bridge, it turns upstream beneath the colourful, craggy flank of Care Scar. Simply remain on this old miners' track all the way along the gill, passing through several gates to reach what was a dressing floor at the old lead mining site. On the right just before the site is stone-arched Lanshaw Level. Ruins and spoil heaps abound as the surroundings open out at the deep enclave of inflowing Bolton Gill.

This is the turning point. Crossing neither beck, turn right up a path above the right bank of the sidestream, looking up into the deep cleft of its valley. Almost immediately a firmer way is met: turn right up this until it levels out beneath an arched level, and here bear right to a gate in the wall just ahead. Leaving the mining scene behind, a grassy path heads away through two more gates. Looking back, the upper reaches of Hebden Gill merge into Grassington Moor, with its smelt mill chimney evident.

The path then rises very gently to be ushered by a wall to a gate at the far end. This admits onto grassy moor, and a wallside path rises to the far end. The conspicuous outline to the left is the grassy dam of Mossy Moor Reservoir, another relic from mining days. Pass through the gate ahead to enter heathery Mossy Moor, and the wallside path rises to a brow to quickly meet a drive to Scar Top House just across to the right. Opposite this point, some 150 paces off the path amidst dense heather is Mossy Moor's modest stone circle, consisting of four major stones and eight in total. In view ahead, meanwhile, is the rocky top of Simon's Seat.

At the wall corner, cross the cattle-grid to follow the track towards Scar Top House, but bear right outside its enclosing wall to a gateway at the bottom. This splendid moment gains the bouldery edge of Care Scar, with a sudden drop back into Hebden Gill. A super little path winds steeply down through bracken to the left of Care Scar's boulders, and continues down to a small gate in the wall below. A thin trod heads off across a green pasture, then slants left to drop with the wall to an outer corner. It then runs on with the wall to a stile at the far end. Advance along a field bottom to a corner stile at the end, then a grassy path slants down above the beck to a stile at the far end. Behind it is a footbridge, but remain on a path along this bank to a row of cottages, passing along the front and up over the old bridge to finish.

At Town Hill, Hebden

4½ miles from Linton

A simple amble through fields and villages, brimful of interest including a rare Wharfe waterfall

Start Linton Falls (SE 001631; BD23 6BQ) National Park car park on Linton Church cul-de-sac

Map OS Explorer 2, Yorkshire Dales South/West

Head along the lane towards the old church, but within a few strides turn right up a walled way that curves left up into a field. Cross to a stile in front of a barn, then behind it to a viewpoint brow on Stickhaw Hill. Resume along the bank top, bearing right to a stile ahead, then across two small fields to the B6160. Go right a few yards to a gate opposite and rise with a wall to a corner. From a stile head away to another then on past an island barn. Maintain this course through further stiles above derelict Linton Camp, rejoining a wall to a corner stile onto a firm track. Drop briefly right, but as it becomes enclosed take a bridle-gate on the right. A fieldside path drops down, through a second fieldside to join an access road. Go ahead and sharp right to enter Linton.

An assortment of buildings stand back from a green: the Fountaine Inn recalls a local benefactor who funded the adjacent 18th century almshouses. Through the green runs Linton Beck, crossed by a ford and road, clapper and packhorse bridges. Leave by a cart track downstream from the other side of the road bridge. This narrows into a footway to emerge into a field: take the branch rising left to a bridge over the old Grassington branch line. Across, head away to a belt of trees, then on with a wall to the B6265. Cross and go left a few strides to head off up a side road. Just past a house, take a stile on the right and head away with a wall. When it departs, continue across this large, sloping pasture to find a stile in a wall converging from the right. Cross towards a farm ahead, using a stile right of a gate onto a road at Grysedale Gate.

Turn right, but before the next house take a stile on the right, dropping to one below and away between wall and streamlet. Opening out, cross to a stile then over a drive bridging a stream to a stile opposite. This hides a slab bridge, from where bear right to a corner stile. Bear right to another further round, and on by a line of trees to the next stile. Turning left up the wallside, cross a stile towards the end and curve right across a large field to a corner stile in front of houses. A few strides down this small enclosure, a stile on the left puts you onto a farm track into Threshfield.

At the Old Hall Inn cross the B6265 to a side road heading away past the green. Joining the B6160, cross and turn right down the footway to a gate on the left. From it a path crosses to bridge the old railway, and a broader track curves down to Threshfield School, a former 17th century grammar school. Turn left on the road the short way to a small gate on the right, and a path doubles back to join the Wharfe alongside a restored turbine house and weir. An access track heads downstream, and as it swings right at a house, advance to Li'l Emily's Bridge ahead. Across, turn left on a snicket to Linton Falls footbridge, a perfect vantage point as the river tumbles over limestone ledges. To finish, double back along the snicket and onto the road just short of the car park.

Linton Falls

3½ miles from Burnsall

Riverbank, fieldpaths and a hidden hamlet beneath Burnsall Fell

Start Village centre (SE 032611; BD23 6BU), car park and seasonal field
Map OS Explorer 2, Yorkshire Dales South/West

Burnsall's setting is one of near perfection, with bridge, green, maypole, church, inn and cottages fusing together into a classic Wharfedale scene. St Wilfred's church dates largely from the 15th century: alongside is the village school, founded in 1602 as one of the earliest grammar schools. Along with the Red Lion Inn, tearooms and WC, the Devonshire Fell Hotel overlooks the village. Join the Wharfe by turning down between the pub and the bridge, and follow a firm path upstream. It soon sees the back of the village, passing below the church and along to a knoll above the gorge of Loup Scar, where the river rushes through an impressive limestone fault. From these spectacular environs the path drops back to the river to run through wooded surroundings to a suspension bridge below Hebden. It celebrated its centenary in 1985, and stands just past the stepping-stones of Hebden Hippings.

Don't cross but take a bridle-gate on the left immediately before the stepping-stones, and a steep path climbs the little bank through Anniversary Wood, planted in 2004 to celebrate 50 years of the National Park. After looking back over this scene, pass through the bridle-gate and ascend a faint grassy path up the field centre to a gate in a wall at the top: Barden Moor looms boldly ahead. The continuing path runs faintly on the wallside heading away, through two further gates in fences. By the time the brow is reached there are good views up-dale beyond Grass Wood. Continue to a gate onto the B6160, where an old stone guidepost features hands pointing to Burnsall, Linton and Kilnsey.

Cross straight over and up the minor Thorpe Lane, leading to Thorpe. On the highest point the Burnsall path is signed off as a walled track on the left, but first advance two minutes further for a look at Thorpe. This farming hamlet has an elusiveness that allegedly kept it hidden from marauding Scots. Romantically titled Thorpe in the Hollow, it shelters between reef knolls and below the overpowering Thorpe Fell. Note the little enclosed green.

Returning to the brow, take the signed path off through a gate and away as a walled track. At its early demise descend a slim field to a small gate in a fence at the right edge of a small wood. Resume away with a wall on your left, and on to a stile in front of a plank bridge on a streamlet. The way rises away in a virtual straight line across three fields to reach the walled track of Badger Lane. A stile opposite resumes the fields' crossing, the immediate brow revealing Burnsall ahead. Dropping to a stile ahead, the way slants right down to a corner stile, and a direct course for Burnsall is set. The church tower is a useful guide, while behind it, Simon's Seat dominates the skyline. More guidance is provided by a tightly bunched series of stiles, designed to test agility in addition to delaying arrival in Burnsall. The village is entered by way of a back yard, turning right along the street into the centre.

The Wharfe at Burnsall

31

WHARFE BELOW BURNSALL

4¹₂ miles from Burnsall

Limestone pastures with big views sandwiched between lovely riverside walking

Start Village centre (SE 032611; BD23 6BU), car park and seasonal field
Map OS Explorer 2, Yorkshire Dales South/West

For a note on Burnsall see page 30. Leave by crossing the Wharfe on the graceful bridge, and quickly turning right through a gate/stile into a big riverside pasture. A path forms to run past WCs to a small gate on a bank above the returning river, and the now firm, enclosed path enjoys a lovely walk downstream. At a stile leave the Wharfe and cross the field towards the farm at Woodhouse. A footbridge takes you over Barben Beck onto the farm drive. Here forsake the river for now (you will return to this point) and turn left on the drive's short run out to a back road.

Cross to a gate and head up a sunken way. Soon a wall forms on the left, and is followed all the way up this splendid green way with a view left across to Hartlington Hall. At the top it becomes enclosed by walls to run along to modern barns. On your left throughout this is the deep side valley of Barben Beck. Left of the barns follow their access track up between walls, emerging to ascend a fieldside to a gate marking a path crossroads. Continue straight up the once-again walled track to a gate at the top into open pasture. Follow the track the short way up to a wall corner above, then go right above the top side of the wall.

Reaching a stile just short of the corner, Simon's Seat looks splendid ahead. Descend the small field (ignore a stile on the left) to a corner wall-stile, then down the wallside as far as a stile in it. Resume on the wall's other side until near the end, then cross the slim pasture to an old wall on your left. Slant down to a gateway in the bottom corner, and a grass track then runs the short way to a gate at the head of an enclosed way. This drops charmingly down onto the road in Appletreewick, emerging alongside the simple church of St John the Baptist, with imposing High Hall opposite.

Turn right down the street past Mock Beggar Hall and along the full length of the village, including its two pubs. The New Inn achieved fame thanks to the enterprising 'no-smoking' policy of a 1970s landlord, while the Craven Arms is named from the family of William Craven, a 'Dick Whittington' character who found fortune in London, becoming Lord Mayor in 1611: also a great local benefactor, he had Burnsall's grammar school built. The pub's 21st century cruck barn is the first in the Dales for probably 300 years.

Continue past Low Hall to a gate sending an enclosed path past a campsite back to the river. Turn right to follow the Wharfe upstream on a delightful, uncomplicated stroll. On emerging from trees at a wooden stump seat with coins embedded, the river makes a big swing to the left. Here the path is deflected right by an intervening wall to enter the farmyard at Woodhouse. This 17th century manor house boasts an attractive mullioned windowed frontage in an equally enviable setting. Passing to the right you reach the point you left early in the walk, so go straight ahead to the footbridge on Barben Beck and retrace the opening half-mile.

Burnsall

3¾ miles from Appletreewick

**Exceptional river scenery
and much of interest around
the environs of Skyreholme**

APPLETREEWICK

Skyreholme

River Wharfe

Howgill

Start *Village centre (SE 053601;
BD23 6DA), limited roadside parking*
Map *OS Explorer 2, Yorkshire Dales South/West*

Appletreewick has several claims to fame, though many will
best remember its delightful name. Here are three halls and two
pubs, from High Hall near the tiny church of St John the Baptist at
the top, to Low Hall at the bottom. Probably the oldest is Mock
Beggar Hall. The Craven Arms is named from the family of William
Craven, a 'Dick Whittington' character who found fortune in
London, becoming Lord Mayor in 1611: a great local benefactor,
he had Burnsall's grammar school and a number of local bridges
built. The pub's 21st century cruck barn is the first in the Dales for
probably 300 years, while the New Inn achieved fame thanks to
the enterprising 'no-smoking' policy of a 1970s landlord.

Leave by heading west out of the village on the Burnsall
road, past the pubs to a gate sending a walled path past a campsite
to the Wharfe. Turn left alongside the river, meeting an early
interruption as a steep, wooded bank deflects the path up wooden
steps before returning to the bank. Now the Wharfe is faithfully
traced through a couple of pastures before entering a delightful
wooded section above the lively river. Emerging into a field at its
far end, the path forsakes the river by bearing left to a gate sending
a track out onto a narrow road at Haugh Bridge.

Across the bridge leave the road in favour of an enclosed
access track left. Beyond a cottage it narrows to rise onto Howgill
Lane at the top, alongside the farm at Howgill. Turn left along the
unsurfaced lane rising past a caravan site at Howgill Lodge, whose
little shop offers refreshments. A little beyond a converted barn an

old milestone set into the wall points the way to 'Patley Bridge 6', indicating the lane's former importance. At this point leave by a gate/stile opposite and follow an old green way along the wallside, first on its right, then its left. After a gateway, with Skyreholme straight ahead, slope down to a stile in the next wall, and continue down to cross a tiny beck at an old wall. With Skyreholme Beck just to the left, advance along the field to a footbridge on it. Just before this, a fine limekiln stands to the right. Over the bridge steps ascend to housing to emerge onto the road at Skyreholme.

Turn left as far as a T-junction alongside a converted chapel that also served as a school, then double back right, steeply uphill with views back to Simon's Seat looming over Skyreholme. Just past a barn take a stile on the left and slant away down the field, quickly revealing a gap-stile in the wall below. This is the first of a string of wall-stiles, indeed the next few can be discerned ahead, guiding a steady slant down across the fields. At the bottom cross a streamlet in a moist dip alongside an old wall, and rise left up the gentle brow to a redundant gap-stile in a short length of wall - Appletreewick is two minutes ahead. All that remains is a direct march across narrow pastures with stiles in line. Emerging via a lawn, cross to one final stile onto an enclosed track. Go left to emerge between houses onto the road at the top of Appletreewick.

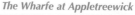

The Wharfe at Appletreewick

3¹₂ miles from Skyreholme

Nussey Green

A limestone ravine is centrepiece to easy rambling amid further interest and views

Trollers Gill

Start Middle Skyreholme (SE 068607; BD23 6DE), limited parking at bridge, also verge parking on road to Parcevall Hall. Access land (not grouse moors).
Map OS Explorer 2, Yorkshire Dales South/West

Parcevall Hall

S

Skyreholme

     Skyreholme is a scattered farming hamlet in its own side valley beneath the dark wall of Simon's Seat. From the junction at the phonebox and seat, cross the bridge and take a small gate on the left to ascend to a gateway at the top corner. Cross the field to another gateway, keeping on with a wall to a corner stile at Ridge End House, and also a tearoom. On your right is the entrance to Parcevall Hall: built over 300 years ago, its beautiful stonework looks across charming gardens to Simon's Seat. Now a diocesan retreat centre, the gardens and woodland are open to the fee-paying public from Easter to October.

     Go left over the wooden bridge onto the public road-end, and take a gate/stile on the right to follow Skyreholme Beck upstream on a good path through further gates. A stile beyond a barn admits to open country, and this colourful enclosure features the grassy retaining wall of a former reservoir made to serve mills at Skyreholme. Up to your left are springtime bluebell banks. The path runs grandly on to another stile before forking in the amphitheatre just short of Trollers Gill, split by the high wedge of Middle Hill. Opt for the right branch which curves into the more open, stony surrounds, passing two springs before at the last moment revealing the secretive entrance to Trollers Gill. Across a wall-stile, set off into the forbidding-looking ravine. Though not particularly tall, the cliffs of this magnificent limestone gorge remain virtually unbroken for some distance. The slim passage between is usually dry, though after rain a substantial stream can fill the floor of the gorge. It is renowned as the home of the legendary 'Barguest', a spectral hound with eyes like saucers.

Crossing a ladder-stile at the end of the main section, simply continue along the shallow, now less dramatic trough, the stream probably re-appearing before you reach another such stile. Just past it, ignore a plank footbridge across the stream and advance on just a little further to a spoil heap and ruined hut at a former lead mining site. Behind the hut is the arched entrance of an old mine level, and here a super green track starts to climb away. To the left note the breached wall of an old dam, while higher up some of the scattered rocks to the left bear cup marks of Bronze Age people (including a flat boulder sporting a dozen distinctive scoops).

This delectable track rises steadily up the open country of Nussey Green to a gate in a wall at the top. Joining the firmer track of Black Hill Road turn right, immediately onto its high point. Ahead is Simon's Seat, which remains a dominant feature. Within a minute the track becomes enclosed at a gate, and a steady descent begins to a junction with another walled way. Turn right down here, quickly becoming surfaced to descend Skyreholme Bank back to the start, with big views across Skyreholme valley.

Trollers Gill

4 miles from Barden

Delectable riverside walking around Barden's historic features

Start *Barden Bridge (SE 052573; BD23 6AS), riverside parking area*
Map *OS Explorer 2, Yorkshire Dales South/West* **or** *Explorer 297, Lower Wharfedale & Washburn Valley*

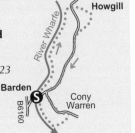

Barden boasts the Wharfe's finest bridge, with a tablet dating its restoration 'at the charge of the whole West Riding' as 1676. Just up the hill is the imposing Barden Tower, built as a hunting lodge by the powerful Cliffords of Skipton Castle. It boasted two famous residents from that family: Henry 'the Shepherd Lord' came in 1485, preferring Barden's peace to Skipton's splendour, while Lady Anne restored the Tower in 1659 and spent much of her final years here. The adjacent chapel serves as a restaurant.

From the parking area turn upstream on a firm path between river and road. As the latter rises away, a gate on the left sends a path onto the riverbank: this is followed all the way upstream to Howgill, with open views on either side. The path soon becomes enclosed by a fence but remains a delight: sandy walls on the opposite bank are the springtime home of nesting sand martins. Eventually the sidestream of Fir Beck deflects you past a farm and out onto a road at Howgill. Cross the road, not the bridge, and take an enclosed track rising away. Beyond a cottage it narrows to meet Howgill Lane at the top, alongside the farm at Howgill. Just a minute to the left is a campsite shop at Howgill Lodge.

Turn right on the firm access road running out to the through road. Go left, and after a slight rise this runs a quiet, level course past several cottages and with super views over the river to Barden Moor. Dropping gently to a junction at Water Gate, bear left for a peaceful ten minutes along Storiths Lane. This runs on past Holme House Farm to arrive at a pair of estate cottages beneath bracken-covered Cony Warren. From a wall-stile on your right descend a permissive path to another stile in the bottom corner, then drop down the bank to the impressive stone Barden Aqueduct. With an early view to Barden Tower popping up above trees, all that remains is to turn upstream for the lovely, all too short riverside walk back to Barden Bridge, which soon beckons ahead.

Opposite: Barden Tower   *Barden Bridge*

3¾ miles from Halton Moor

A walk entirely on heather moorland, on a rocky fringe of Barden Moor

Start Top of Embsay-Barden road (SE 037553; BD23 6AR), lay-bys
Map OS Explorer 2, Yorkshire Dales South/West • *Open Access land, no dogs: see page 4*

With its sweeping views and open moorland, the summit of the Embsay-Barden road is a popular motorists' halt. From the main lay-by follow the roadside verge eastwards the short way to drop to the cattle-grid off the moor. Ahead are Lower Barden Reservoir and the majestic sweep of Simon's Seat across the Wharfe. Don't cross the grid but turn right on a wallside track along the moor-edge, down through the little gulch of How Gill. Ahead, Beamsley Beacon and Rombalds Moor frame Wharfedale's lower reaches. The track swings right to run to the head of grassy Moor Lane above Halton East. Don't take the gate onto it but remain on a grassy path along the foot of bracken-clad moor. This splendid little path shortly slants up beneath the substantial boulders of Low Crag, short-cutting a bend of the wall to squeeze up between wall and scarp back onto the moorland road.

Go briefly left, and before the cattle-grid turn right up a grassy path parallel with the wall. The path winds up to join the wall, but soon doubles back sharply right to rise the short way to the base of an extensive old quarry at High Crag. Set back and unseen above this is an OS column atop Halton Height: at the right end of the quarry rises a distinctive pinnacle. Remain on the path as it runs left to expire beneath the far end of the cliff. A thin trod takes up the running, quickly levelling out to approach the wall again. Resume west onto the brow, the wood ending and views opening out ahead to the impressive profile of Embsay Crag and more of Barden Moor's expanse. Simply trace this thin but good wallside path, soon dropping gently down to a gate/stile at Eastby Gate, just short of a steeper drop to Heugh Gill.

Turn sharp right here to remain on the moor, a grass path veering slightly left to the first of a row of grouse butts. The now broader path rises gently to shadow this dead-straight line of stone butts to the far end. Here a broader way comes in from the left, quickly becoming a firmer track. Ahead, more of the moor opens out, Simon's Seat looms dramatically over Wharfedale, and the lower reservoir is outspread below. Slanting down to the right you rapidly arrive between two shooters' cabins at Hutchen Gill Head.

Leave the track here and bear left past the second cabin, where a short-lived, grassy trough leads to cross the breached dam of an old reservoir. The trod continues through heather to quickly meet the firm track of the Rylstone-Bolton Abbey bridleway. Turn right on this, dropping down to absorb the track from the cabins, and your way leads across the moor under Halton Height. This relaxing stroll allows you to fully absorb the spectacular views across the moor as it returns you unfailingly to the start. Towards the end, just before a gate, take a more inviting path slanting right - the true course of the bridleway and nicer underfoot. It rises slightly then runs on, keeping left at any forks and crossing the brow to emerge onto the road opposite the main parking area.

Looking down on Barden Lower Reservoir

3¾ miles from Bolton Abbey

Excellent paths through outstanding river and woodland scenery

Start Cavendish Pavilion (SE 077552; BD23 6AN), car park off B6160 just north of Bolton Abbey, turn by memorial fountain
Map OS Explorer 2, Yorkshire Dales South/West *or* Explorer 297, Lower Wharfedale & Washburn Valley

Barden Bridge

River Wharfe

The Strid

Strid Wood

Cavendish Pavilion **S**

This delectable section of the Wharfe is part of the Duke of Devonshire's Bolton Abbey estate, and a combination of largely permissive paths allows good access to both banks: this splendid 19th century path network has been well maintained ever since. Strid Wood is a hugely popular riverside habitat where man and nature happily co-exist, and the importance of the woodland for birds and plants is recognised by designation as a Site of Special Scientific Interest. Springtime bluebells add a beautiful carpet to the woodland floor, though at any time of year this is pure delight.

From the Pavilion with its refreshments, gift shop and WC, cross the river bridge and take the path upstream. At a bridle-gate into trees it forks: remain on the riverbank, soon crossing a footbridge adjacent to Posforth Gill road bridge. The path clings to the river until faced with a sustained pull to the wood top, where a well-sited rest house awaits. This up-market seat occupies the first of several very well-chosen viewpoints, in this case a lovely picture of the river downstream. Hereafter, easy walking ensues on a magnificent terrace, and two near-neighbouring benches offer surprise cameos of The Strid framed by foliage.

Shortly after, another classic moment reveals the lively High Strid in a contrastingly open setting. The path leaves the wood at a wall gateway to slant down to the river at an impressive stone aqueduct. Built to carry a water pipeline from Nidderdale's reservoirs to the taps of Bradford, it carries a path which offers a brief view of Barden Tower upstream. Also the walk's turning point, cross it and descend wooden steps to begin the return on the path downstream. Entering Strid Wood on a sidestream footbridge remain on the main path, ignoring an early fork to the Strid car park and tearoom.

Shortly after a brief pull to a seat the path forks: keep left, another path soon coming back in and then rising to its high point. Just past here, and with The Strid directly below, take a thinner but still firm branch left high above a rock pinnacle - the Hawkstone - to drop to the famous Strid itself. The Strid is the focal point of the wood, as the Wharfe is forced through a long, narrow gritstone channel of great depth. Lives have been lost here in attempts to leap the foaming waters, while many decades ago visitors could arrive in style, by wagonette from the railway station. The broad carriageway created for those early visitors now leads gently all the way to the Cavendish Pavilion, a couple of late branches offering closer spells with the river at Lud Stream Islands.

The Strid

4½ miles from Bolton Abbey

A delectable side valley leads to a more open moorland return

Start Cavendish Pavilion (SE 077552; BD23 6AN), car park off B6160 just north of Bolton Abbey, turn by fountain
Map OS Explorer 2, Yorkshire Dales South/West *or* 297, Lower Wharfedale & Washburn Valley

• Open Access land, no dogs: see page 4

    The Cavendish Pavilion stands on the riverbank at the entrance to Strid Wood, with refreshments, gift shop and WC. Leave by crossing the wooden bridge on the Wharfe and taking a broad path upstream. Through a bridle-gate at the end savour superb river scenery before taking the right branch climbing to a back road. Turn left up this, with an immediate parallel path on its top side rising the short way to the road's high point. Here take a gate on the right and bear left onto an inviting green track past Waterfall Cottage. From a gate at the end a firmer track winds along to terminate at a pond in the Valley of Desolation. The inappropriate title refers to the aftermath of a great storm in 1826.

    Posforth Gill is just in front, and here you have a brief choice. Simplest option turns right on the grass along the rim of the steep drop to the beck, rising past a small wood and on above the beck to quickly reach a footbridge. The best path makes a short drop to the beck from the pond, then upstream to a footbridge. On the other bank you enjoy a super view of a beautiful waterfall as you climb past it. Just above, the path runs on to pass a footbridge bringing the direct path in. Re-united, the path continues more narrowly along the valley floor, soon reaching a fork. Take the main path rising left to a bridle-gate into Laund Pasture Plantation.

A broad track ascends rapidly to the far end of the trees, where a gate admits into open country at a moorland corner. The dome of Earl Seat is on the left, with the Simon's Seat path distinct ahead.

Two firm tracks head away: ignore that to the left, and take the wallside one straight ahead. Within five minutes leave in favour of an inviting green track bearing right with the wall the short way down to cross Agill Beck. A stone trough sits on the grassy bank, a nice spot to linger. Leaving moorland, for now, at the gate/stile behind follow a gentle green track across a couple of pastures to the old barn of Agill House. Continue to a gateway beyond it and then a gate, from where a fenceside track runs above tree-lined Hudson Gill. Dropping to a concrete crossing, double back right up the other side to a gate. It runs on through a gateway and swings left with the wall to the secluded old farm of Broadshaw.

Pass between the buildings and follow the access track down to a ford and footbridge, then up through a gate and away over a brow to a cattle-grid in a wall to re-enter open country. Rising through heather the walk's summit is gained at 1033ft/315m on Hammerthorn Hill. The track quickly drops to reach Hammerthorn Gate, meeting another track coming in from the left to leave the moor. Through the gate resume down the stony track, with Bolton Priory seen on the valley floor. The track drops unfailingly down through fields to the attractive farmhouse of Bolton Park. Passing to the right of the buildings its drive leads down to the back road, re-crossing the bridge to finish.

Waterfall,
Posforth Gill

4 miles from Bolton Abbey

A riverside stroll in fine surrounds: central is Upper Wharfedale's most iconic building

Start Village centre (SE 071539; BD23 6EX), car park
Map OS Explorer 2, Yorkshire Dales South/West *or* Explorer 297, Lower Wharfedale & Washburn Valley

Bolton Abbey is the name for the tiny village whose showpiece is more correctly Bolton Priory. Spread around are shop, tearoom, antiquarian bookshop, WC and a splendid tithe barn. From the car park follow the short road out to a triangular green at the B6160. Cross to a gate at the 'Hole in the Wall', and a firm path descends into the priory grounds. On your left before the priory is Bolton Hall, dating from the 17th century. Follow the main path as far as a footbridge on the Wharfe, and without crossing, turn downstream. A long, pleasant pasture leads all the way to Bolton Bridge. As it appears ahead, the Devonshire Arms Hotel appears to the right, and a kissing-gate offers a detour to it. The old road is joined at the shapely bridge, left in peace since completion of the 1994 by-pass. A steam railway from Embsay has seen Bolton Abbey's restored station back in use, a long half-mile along the A59.

Cross the bridge, and just beyond a cottage turn left along an enclosed pathway before Red Lion Farm to enter a riverside pasture. As the Wharfe is neared the grassy way is deflected above a wooded bank, and from a stile at the end it drops back down to cross long flat pastures parallel with the river. After a tiny stream and a stile another wooded bank intervenes. A steep field is climbed, remaining with the left-hand fence to a stile at the end. Now go briefly left along the bank top to reach a superb high-level vantage point for the priory.

Just past a stile is a path junction. Slant down the bank to a T-junction, where the right branch immediately slants back up. The solid path quickly enters woodland, running a high-level course near the top of the wooded bank. At the end it drops down to emerge onto a narrow road descending to ford Pickles Beck, with an adjacent footbridge. On the other side a gate sends a riverbank path upstream the short way to a broad wooden bridge crossing to the Cavendish Pavilion with refreshments, gift shop and WC.

From the Pavilion set off left along the drive, but quickly bear left into the car park and follow an access road close by the river. When the track ends a path goes on through a gate, then with the priory beyond a river bend, the path swings right to climb to steps emerging onto the road at a big fountain. This commemorates Lord Frederick Cavendish, assassinated in Dublin in 1882: Cavendish is the family name of the Dukes of Devonshire, owners of the estate. Turn left to quickly reach a gate into the priory grounds. The imposing ruin of Bolton Priory dates from 1154, and was built by Augustinian canons who moved here from nearby Embsay. At the Dissolution the nave was spared, and remains to this day the parish church. After a leisurely exploration, advance on to rejoin the outward path to return to the village.

Bolton Abbey

47

4¼ miles from Hazlewood

Rich variety in and above the side valley of Kex Beck

Start Hill End (SE 094540; BD23 6JQ), lay-by on old road off A59 (200 yards below a snack bar lay-by on main road)

Map OS Explorer 2, Yorkshire Dales South/West or Explorer 297, Lower Wharfedale & Washburn Valley

Storiths   Hazlewood **S**

New Hall

Howgill Side

Beamsley   Deerstones

     Return to the main road and cross with care to embrace the colourful valley of Kex Beck beneath Beamsley Beacon. From a gate a surfaced track transforms into a green way dropping to a gate accessing a footbridge on the beck. Turning downstream a thin path enters new tree plantings, and is quickly deflected to rise with a wall to Low Howgill. Follow the drive out above Howgill Side and on to Ling Chapel Farm, with Beamsley Beacon's bouldery edge high above. Emerging onto open moor, turn right to cross the farm drive and down to a fence-gate. A grassy path descends the reedy moorland, and through a bridle-gate slants down through colourful terrain into the steep-sided environs of Kex Beck.

     Across a footbridge a grassy path slants up to the houses at Deerstones. Without entering, go left before the first house to a gate sending a grassy path along the bank top, soon slanting back down through trees to the beck. Just beyond, a stile takes you out of the trees to resume downstream through two pastures split by a stile/gate. At a narrow section amid scrub, take the path slanting right up the modest bank to an old stile. Head away with the wall, through another stile and along to a bridle-gate back onto the A59. Cross to Beamsley Hospital opposite. Through an arch, a second archway flanked by six almshouses reveals the roundhouse. From a central chapel seven individual rooms radiate: it is now a holiday let. A tablet in the archway beneath the Clifford arms tells its origins:

This almshouse was founded by that excellent lady Margaret Russell Countess of Cumberland, wife to George Clifford, third Earl of Cumberland 1593, and was more perfectly finished by her only child Lady Anne Clifford, now Countess Dowager of Pembrooke, Dorsett and Montgomery. God's name be praised.

Back outside, a path rises past a postbox to a section of old road. A rough road immediately goes back sharply left between houses to run by Struff Wood to New Hall Farm. Passing through a gate with the farm just ahead, turn right along the wallside, then left at the corner to a bridle-gate at the end. With the farmhouse to your left, cross to a wall-stile ahead, then left across a bumpy enclosure to the lower of two wall-stiles. Cross to a stile ahead, then slant up to the far end of the field. From a stile/gate follow the right-hand wall, through a stile at the end to rise to another onto a lane in Storiths. Turn right up the short access road onto Storiths Lane. To the left is Back 'o th' Hill Farm with refreshments.

Turn right here for a few minutes, and after Storiths House Farm but before some barns, take a stile on the left and slant right down the field to a stile in a short wall section at the bottom. Over a slab bridge a path slants right to a top corner stile, from where slant left up the field to a wall-stile just short of the top. This puts you onto a back road through the hamlet of Hazlewood. Turn left, passing the old schoolhouse of 1832 and absorbing the by-passed old road to reach the start point.

Beamsley Hospital

4 miles from Langbar

Entirely moorland walking to a popular mini-mountain landmark

Start Beacon Hill (SE 091521; LS29 0EX), parking area on Beamsley side just beneath road summit

Map OS Explorer 297, Lower Wharfedale & Washburn Valley

• Open Access land, no dogs: see page 4

From the parking area ascend the short way to the road summit, and on past a couple of houses to where it swings sharply downhill. Here advance straight on an access road, passing an old school and onto open moor. Your route is Badgers Gate, once patronised by travelling corn dealers, or 'badgers'. Views look across the valley to Rombalds Moor, with Beamsley Beacon back up to your left. When the wall drops away the road forks: remain on the upper branch across the moor to end at Wards End. Here a thin path branches left to run on above a wall, dropping to a moist dip. Just past this the wall swings sharp right, but the path bears left to briefly rise to a path crossroads at an old stone guidepost on Middleton Moor. This records the miles to Skipton (6), Ot(t)ley (5) and Knar(e)sb(o)rough (11). Turn left here, a splendid broad path traversing the ridge on a gentle descent to a gate in a wall.

Don't pass through but take the inviting green shooters' track left, rising dead-straight with the wall all the way to a gate in a bend at the top. Though the track passes above, instead take a softer track rising left to a grouse butt. It then swings right to trace a long line of butts, and soon levelling out, it later narrows to path width. After the last butt it continues a gentle rise across the moor, initially briefly moist but soon improving. When it swings sharp left to commence a level course, instead continue straight uphill, within two minutes meeting a broad, well-worn path just short of the ridge top. Go left on a steady rise to The Old Pike: as this appears, so does Beamsley Beacon beyond. At 1312ft/400m, its top is marked by a group of rocks in the heather.

As the beacon is lower, your 'ascent' is actually a descent! Simply follow the broad ridge-path along to the popular landmark of Beamsley Beacon. At 1289ft/393m the OS column is dwarfed by a huge pile of stones, and bears a memorial to the Canadian crew of a Lancaster bomber that crashed on these slopes in 1945. The massive cairn is the remains of a Bronze Age mound, thought to be the burial place of a local chieftain. Just two centuries ago a beacon was manned here during the Napoleonic wars, and foundations of the beacon guard's house survive.

An outstanding moorland panorama, anti-clockwise from the north-east, features Kex Gill Moor, Rocking Moor, Hazlewood Moor, Simon's Seat, Earl Seat, Barden Moor, Flasby Fell, Skipton Moor, Rombalds Moor, Otley Chevin and back to Blubberhouses Moor. Westwards are Lancashire's Pendle Hill, Longridge Fell and Bowland moors, though finest feature is the bird's-eye view over the Beamsley and Bolton Bridge area. Resume on the well-worn descent path, soon joining the crest of a rocky edge on your right. Towards the bottom a broad path forks right, dropping down to meet a wall that leads down to a track just short of the parking area. If missed, simply continue a couple of minutes further down the main path, squeezed between walls down onto the road top.

Looking north from Beamsley Beacon

4¾ miles from Addingham

A lovely riverside stroll to an historic Quaker meeting house, extensive views

Start Village centre (SE 079497; LS29 0LY), Memorial Hall car park
Map OS Explorer 297, Lower Wharfedale & Washburn Valley

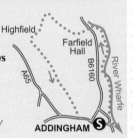

Addingham's busy street supports pubs, tearooms and shops. Turn towards Ilkley, and near the village foot go left on Church Street to a junction with North Street. Turning left, a path drops right at an early bend. As the right branch descends to a bridge on the Wharfe, fork left upstream above the river. Shortly reaching a fork drop right, closer to the river to reach converted High Mill. This deflects you left into a courtyard and ahead to a gate into a caravan park. Head away along the drive, but soon after bridging a sidestream, a path returns you to the Wharfe at a weir.

The river now leads unfailingly up-dale, with a kissing-gate taking you into open countryside. After a couple of fields you are forced up above a steep, wooded bank. From a stile at the top, the path runs on above trees, and from a stile at the end drops steeply back to the river. After further delightful rambling, another wooded bank intervenes beyond a ladder-stile. At the top a stile leads into trees to skirt a house to join the B6160 at Lobwood. Cross to a kissing-gate accessing Farfield Friends' Meeting House, a Quaker building of 1689. Behind it turn right on the old Lobwood House drive. Pass through a gate and up to join the drive just above. At this fork take the left one, swinging round into Farfield Livery.

Remain on the firm track rising past stables and running to an old rail underpass, through which it runs right to a gate into a field. Slant diagonally up to a wall-stile above Eller Carr Wood. Now more level, maintain this line up into the field centre, where double back left up to a stile in the left-hand wall before reaching the top. Stunning views feature the Bolton Abbey scene. Head away with the wall to merge with a track at the end. Through the stile/gate advance to where wall and track curve right. Ignoring a dangerous wall-stile, leave the track at the wall-end before the clump of trees to bear left across the field to a wall-stile. Cross towards Highfield Farm, passing an outer wall corner to lead on the short way to the left of the farm. A wall-stile ahead puts you into a field in front of the farm, where bear left to a gate onto a golf course. With a wall over to the right, advance straight on through scattered trees near the edge of the course. Further, a path runs through more trees to a stile temporarily off the course. A slender pasture leads on past Highfield House to a stile back onto the course. Continue straight down, passing a stone shed before an inviting path runs through rough grassland and a few trees. Passing a small pond on your right, you find a stile off the course at the bottom.

Continue down an inviting wooded avenue. With the ruined barn of High Laithe to your right, the path continues parallel with an overgrown sunken way on the left. This remains a lovely course, through a stile and down again to one on the left before the bottom corner. With the now serviceable lane alongside, remain parallel until a kissing-gate at the bottom gives entry to it. This runs on to a road, where go left and then right on Sugar Hill to finish.

River Wharfe above Addingham

4³4 miles from Ilkley

A colourful ramble with a wooded gill and bluebell woods sandwiched between riverbank walking

Start Old Bridge (SE 112480; LS29 9EU), roadside parking
Map OS Explorer 297, Lower Wharfedale & Washburn Valley

From the town cross the bridge and take a riverside path left through greenery to emerge onto a road. Cross and go left for a steep slant up suburban Owler Park Road to a bend at the top. From a stile on the left a good path runs through Owler Park Wood with springtime bluebells. A stile at the end puts you into a field: across it, veer right to a streamlet crossing and bridle-gate back into trees. The path scales a little bank to a stile back out, over a simple footbridge and on a field above Low Austby. Advance to a stile with a gate just beyond, soon tracing a wall along. Big views look left to Ilkley Moor, as indeed they do for most of this walk. After a wall-stile a fence takes over, leading to a stile/gate at the end onto a rough track dropping the few yards onto a narrow road. Go briefly right into Nesfield, with its postman's shelter on a tiny green.

Turn right here, and straight on through a gate as the access road swings left. A pleasant access track rises with the wooded gill to approach a lone house at Dean. Don't advance to it but take a clear path bearing left shortly after a farm set back on your left. The path rises through bracken to an early gate above Dean. Gently rising through dense bracken, in the upper half the path traces the left-hand edge as the gill takes more shape. Ultimately reaching a gate at the top, a little path rises onto a driveway at some houses. Follow this right to Upper Austby, straight on through the yard and swinging left out onto a road.

Go right on a near-level course until just past a line of pines on the right, a gate sends a fieldside track through a gate below. From one at the bottom it continues pleasantly down to join a drive. In woodland just to the right is Calvary, created around 1850, with carved stones representing the Stations of the Cross lining a path to a grotto. Resume on the access road, dropping past cottages to swing left above 400-year old Middleton Lodge onto Hardings Lane. Go briefly left to a junction, where to your left stands an old carved guidepost whose hands point to destinations include Rip(p)on. Here branch right along the Middleton lane, and past a solitary house take a stile on the right. Slant left down the field to a stile into Middleton Woods, decorated in spring by a rich carpet of bluebells.

An immediate fork is the first of many twists and turns: go right, then immediately left at another fork to descend a little before running left to a junction. Keep right on the main path, descending a steep flight of stone steps, then down more gently. Towards the bottom it runs left over a tiny footbridge just beyond a crossroads with a thinner path. At the next fork keep right, dropping down a finger of woodland between gardens to emerge onto a suburban avenue. Go briefly left to descend steps to playing fields at the open-air pool. Pass the pool on your left to cross a road, on past the rugby ground to the riverbank. Go right to cross the new bridge to return by the Wharfe to the Old Bridge.

Middleton Woods

4¼ miles from Ilkley

A classic stroll on a windswept moorland edge

Addingham Moorside — Cragg House — Briery Wood — ILKLEY — S — Heber's Ghyll — Swastika Stone — Windgate Nick — Addingham High Moor

Start *Heber's Ghyll (SE 100472; LS29 9RQ) almost at end of Heber's Ghyll Drive, reached via Grove Road from town centre, roadside parking*
Map *OS Explorer 297, Lower Wharfedale & Washburn Valley*

Leave the road on the Ilkley side of the bridge on Heber's Ghyll, on a path bearing right into trees to a footbridge at the gill foot. This well-surfaced path rises alongside tumbling Heber's Ghyll, which is re-crossed numerous times during a steep ascent before arriving at a stone shelter. The right-hand path runs a few strides to an iron gate onto the foot of Heber Moss. Go right on the wallside path, through a small gate above the wood corner. Visible ahead are railings guarding the Swastika Stone on Woodhouse Crag. The little path crosses a streamlet and slants left the short way up through bilberry bushes. Keep left at an early fork to soon emerge on a broader path running right the short way to the Swastika Stone. Thought to date from the Bronze Age, the less obvious carving is on the main rock, that at the front being a replica.

The path now sets off on a well-defined course across the moor, rising ever gradually through stiles to a cluster of windswept larches. Through a crumbling wall beyond them, a better-defined edge soon re-forms on Piper's Crag. Some boulders to your right bear Bronze Age cup & ring markings. Small metal gates in intervening walls punctuate this classic march under Addingham High Moor, with big views over Addingham and Bolton Abbey to hazy heights up Wharfedale. Not long after the isolated Noon Stone, a final gate sees the path enjoy a short spell in heather away from the edge. Soon a cairn is reached at a path crossroads at Windgate Nick.

Here, just yards short of the edge's highest point, descend through the aptly-named Nick into a former quarry. The main path bears right below the cliffs, through a rash of stones and down a grassy groove to a stile in the wall. A grassy path descends the reedy pasture below, and across a moist area it drops to a stile in the bottom corner. A wall then leads down through gorse bushes to a stile onto Moorside Lane serving Addingham Moorside. Turn right to its terminus at a gate in front of Cragg House Farm.

Don't descend to it but take the access track straight ahead, on through a corner gate and along field bottoms to two cottages. On again, it terminates at Hardwick House, to the right of which a short path runs to a hand-gate into reedy pasture. Cross the bottom the short way to a wall-stile, and head away with a wall on your right. A path briefly forms above a stand of trees, then advance to a wall-stile just ahead. From another just beyond it, slant gently down across a larger pasture to a wall-stile at an old gateway above the houses at Briery Wood Farm. A hollowed path drops to the rear of the buildings and along the driveway out, quickly meeting the end of Heber's Ghyll Drive at a gateway. From a small gateway to the right follow an excellent parallel path along the base of Bracken Wood, profuse with springtime bluebells. This runs unfailingly back to the start.

Ilkley from Heber Moss

57

4³4 miles from Ilkley

Exploring lesser known settlements across the Wharfe from Ilkley

Start Parish church
(SE 116478; LS29 9DS),
car parks nearby
Map OS Explorer 297, Lower Wharfedale & Washburn Valley

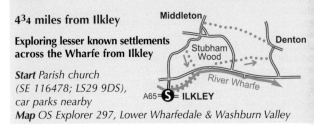

Ilkley is the highest town on the Wharfe, a perfect stepping-stone between industrial conurbations and the Yorkshire Dales. All Saints' church has a 500-year old tower, but is best known for its Anglo-Saxon crosses, also a well-preserved effigy of 14th century knight Adam de Middleton. The church covers part of the site of the Roman fort of Verbeia, built around 79 AD: a small section of preserved wall survives. Also by the church is the splendid 16th century Manor House. From the church descend New Brook Street towards the Wharfe, and before the bridge turn down steps on the left to a riverside path. Follow this under the road bridge of 1904, and continue downstream on this urban path nudged by suburbia onto a quieter section to a suspension footbridge.

Cross to the Denton road under Stubham Wood and resume downstream, using some verges parallel with the Wharfe passing a drive to Nell Bank. Just beyond, at a stile on the left, cross to the far field corner, then along a fieldside below trees to a kissing-gate onto Carters Lane. Take the drive to Beckfoot Farm opposite, and crossing a bridge into the yard, go straight ahead past the garden. Turn left outside the wall, along a path on a grassy brow to a small gate in the boundary wall. Cross and bear right outside West Park Wood. Beyond two stiles/gates a track out of the wood runs through two further fields to a gate/stile onto a road. Turn up it to the quiet backwater of Denton, its old school stood back from a tiny green. To the right past Home Farm is the splendid Denton Hall of 1770 currently an events venue. Before it is St Helen's church of 1776.

Turn left at the tiny green to quickly find a stile/gate onto a short enclosed track left. From a stile/gate at the end advance with a fence to the top of West Park Wood. A stile/gate keep you out of the trees, running along the top to one giving access into the far end, as the wood starts to curve right. Path and bridge combine to see you out via a stile. Cross a large, sloping field enveloped by woodland to a stile into trees, and a path descends to a footbridge on Bow Beck and steeply up the other bank. Bearing right at a kink at the top, the path traces the wood-edge. On leaving the trees at a stile the way traces a fence rising gently away. Interrupted by a farm track and another stile, the next stile sends steps down to a tiny footbridge, then cross to a stile onto Hunger Hill Lane.

Go left to a crossroads at Middleton, and straight over down Curly Hill. Beyond suburbia take a stile on the left into Stubham Wood, decorated in spring by a rich carpet of bluebells. Take the central of three paths heading away, slanting gently down and running more to the left to cross a broader path in a clearing. Your continuation is a splendid thinner path that slants faithfully down to meet a broad path just above the bottom of the wood. This drops down to a kissing-gate onto the road opposite the suspension bridge. For a different finish go briefly right on the footway, quickly joining the grassy riverbank to trace it back upstream to the bridge.

At Denton

4¹2 miles from Ilkley

A wealth of moorland landmarks

Start Keighley Road (SE 110468; LS29 9RB), parking areas where moor-foot continuation of Wells Road bridges Spicey Gill
Map OS Explorer 297, Lower Wharfedale & Washburn Valley

• *Open Access: dogs on leads, March to July*

From the near end of the parking area on the Ilkley side of the bridge, a firm path contours away through moorland undergrowth. Its splendid course loses a little height and absorbs a path from the left, but remains foolproof as White Wells is seen ahead. Joining a stony road, it rises right to White Wells. This 18th century cottage is a monument to Ilkley's early spa days, built by Squire Middleton as a bath-house for townsfolk to dip in pure moorland spring water. It is now a visitor centre with refreshments: inside is a deep, circular pool hollowed from rock and fed by a cold mineral spring. By this stage you have massive views over the town to bleak moors opposite.

Now fully embracing Ilkley Moor, behind the cottage a stepped path climbs to meet a broader one, rising left and running to a fork below a small plantation. Bear right up a stone staircase above the onset of Ilkley Crags overlooking Rocky Valley. Just above the start of the crags the way eases, and the path bears right to a cross-paths. Go straight across to advance on up the open moor, soon arriving at tiny Backstone Beck where a lesser path comes in from the left. Across, the path acquires a flagged surface, a long level section preceding a short pull towards the 1833 boundary stoop of Lanshaw Lad. Only a thin path climbs to it as the main path bears left to level out, and the flags end. This is the turning point, but the path runs two minutes further to the Bronze Age Twelve Apostles stone circle overlooking both Wharfedale and Airedale.

Your onward route retraces steps and turns off along the flagged path behind Lanshaw Lad. This grand stride runs a lengthy course set back from the minor edge of White Crag Moss. At a dip it leaves the edge to slant left, rising gently to reach the OS column on Rombalds Moor summit at 1319ft/402m. The view across the valley stretches from Buckden Pike and Great Whernside at the dalehead down to Simon's Seat, Beamsley Beacon, Menwith Hill, Almscliff Crag and Otley Chevin. Resume on the flagged path angling towards the ridge wall. En route, small boulders include the Puddle Stone, featuring the work of poet Simon Armitage. Meeting the Thimble Stones at the wall, the path runs on with it to Whetstone Gate (locally known as Keighley Gate), through which is the surfaced terminus of the road climbing from the Aire Valley.

Turn right on the rough road, and within five minutes you see Cowper's Cross set 50 yards back: a little path breaks off to view it. Resume down the old road to a green knoll above the amphitheatre of Grainings Head. Just yards further as it swings left, take a path straight ahead, down through bracken close by Spicey Gill. Passing above an old quarry rim on your right, then over a contouring path, it drops quite steeply to rejoin the now surfaced road. Continue down to finish, passing on your left an old stone guidepost with carved hands pointing to Keighley and Ilkley.

The Twelve Apostles

4¾ miles from Ilkley

A rich tapestry of fascinating moorland landmarks

Start Cow & Calf Rocks (SE 132467; LS29 8BT) *popular moorland car park with cafe opposite Cow & Calf Hotel* **Map** OS Explorer 297, Lower Wharfedale & Washburn Valley • *Open Access: dogs on leads, March to July*

Perched on the moor high above Ilkley, the Cow & Calf Rocks are a celebrated Yorkshire landmark. This is a popular climbing area, while below the Cow, its offspring the Calf offers an easy angled scramble. Take the main flagged path from the car park towards the rocks, but leave before them on another flagged path slanting left. This rises to a path junction, turning right the short way to a major cross-paths on the brow. Turn left on the broad, level path. After 150 yards keep on over a cross-path, and after a further 100 yards, a fork is reached immediately after another path junction. Take that bearing right, before long starting a gentle slant beneath the distinctive Pancake Stone to soon gain a modest edge.

Here begins a splendid march along Burley Moor edge, with big views across to Middleton and Denton Moors, also Almscliff Crag and Otley Chevin. The path drops gently to cross a streamlet and up again to a wall corner to continue by the wall. Dropping gently after the wall turns off, you arrive above a steep drop to Coldstone Beck. The path descends to cross the stony stream, then doubles back left to a fork: take the rougher upper one to emerge onto the level. Head away, ignoring a very early left branch to soon reach a cross-paths. Turn right, rising away before easing out, over a cross-track and up again to arrive at Lower Lanshaw Dam. The path continues along its right side before a final rise onto a broad track in front of the Grubstones, with a wooden cabin to the left. Big views over lower Airedale greet you here.

Turn briefly right on the track to a dip, where a grassy path bears right down to High Lanshaw Dam. Across the outflow and embankment, drop left on a path to stepping-stones over a marsh, then rise gently away to a knoll at the start of Lanshaw Delves. Here leave the broad, stony path ahead in favour of the inviting left branch. The delves are a distinctive line of small quarry hollows on a glacial moraine: the second of many contains the fallen Lanshaw Lass boundary stone. A super path runs the full length, at the end crossing briefly moister moorland to meet the flagged Dick Hudson's path. Turn right for a rapid descent across Ilkley Moor, until crossing Backstone Beck the flags end and the path forks. Keep to the left one rising briefly before continuing a steady descent. Soon reaching a major cross-paths Ilkley re-appears: go straight over as it drops left to the eastern rim of Ilkley Crags.

Escape the stony descent by turning right on a contrastingly inviting grassy path above the substantial crags, with great views into Rocky Valley below. This rises gently all the way, at the end merging into the broad path from that previous cross-paths. Dropping to cross bouldery Backstone Beck, take the left-hand of two main paths heading away: it drops to a modest hollow and back up the short way to the crest of the Cow & Calf Rocks. Bear right along the top, past a gaping climbers' quarry to a firmer path. Quickly reaching the cross-paths at the end of the rocks, retrace steps left to finish.

Cow & Calf Rocks

4¼ miles from Grimwith

An uncomplicated circuit of a vast sheet of water, its moorland surrounds adding a sense of space and colour

Start Water company car park off B6265 east of Hebden (SE 063640; BD23 5ED) **Map** OS Explorer 2, Yorkshire Dales South/West

Gate Up Gill
Grimwith Moor
Grimwith House
Grimwith Reservoir
Grimwith Fell

Grimwith Reservoir was built in 1884, and enlarged a century later into Yorkshire's largest expanse of inland water. Below the car park/WC is a sailing club, while in late summer the surrounding heather moors make a fine backdrop. From the car park head east on the track rising away. Beyond a gate the wall drops away, after which an inviting path branches left, slanting down the heathery bank to run above the shoreline. At the end it rejoins the track at the restored cruck-framed and heather-thatched High Laithe Barn. Resume along the hard track past Grimwith House and a colourful side dam. The track winds round onto the northern shore, past a shooting house up to the right and the ruin of Gate Up on the left. Across the dam is the Barden Moor skyline.

When the track finally turns up to a barn, keep straight on a broad, firm path through bracken. This is the finest section as you head towards the attractive ravines of Gate Up Gill and Blea Gill. Before reaching them a track comes back in, and bridges each in turn. The track emerges from the far corner to lead down the west side, a belt of trees masking the reservoir. A brief rise to a brow enjoys a good view over the lake: here take a path left through a gate, down past a barn and on past a small wood. At the end a walled track runs to a gate at the western end of the great dam. A pleasant walk along the top of the relatively unobtrusive grassy embankment leads back to the road just short of the car park.